"O to set foot on Aphrodite's island, on Cyprus,
haunted by the Loves,
who enchant Brief life with sweetness;"

Euripides, "The Bacchae".

CYPRUS IN COLOUR

First published in May 1987 by
K. P. Kyriakou (Books & Stationery) Ltd
P.O. Box 159 - Limassol - Cyprus.
☎ 05-368508 Fax 05-371706.

Distributed by **KYRIAKOU BOOKSHOPS**

This book was conceived, edited and produced by
Georgios Kyriakou.

Credits

Photography   Vassos Stylianou Studios
Design   Ecastica Advertising and Design Ltd
Text   John Vickers

Acknowledgements

The publishers would like to thank sincerely the
following for their valuable help in the preparation of
this book:
The Cyprus Museum, Department of Antiquities,
Folk Art Museum, The Abbot of the Royal Kykkos
Monastery, Father Stylianos, Mr. George Achilles,
Mr. Pilavakis.

ISBN 9963-7617-1-2

45

CONTENTS

PUBLISHERS' NOTE

This first edition of CYPRUS IN COLOUR is an illustrated guide to the major part of the island. It cannot include the many attractions of the whole of Cyprus due to the continuing illegal presence of Turkish troops which invaded the island on July 20th, 1974 and attempted to destroy the Republic of Cyprus. Their military intervention caused heavy loss of life and almost half of the Greek Cypriot population became refugees in their own country, forced to flee from the northern occupied part of Cyprus to the government-controlled southern part. Since then Turkey has persistently refused to withdraw its armed forces despite repeated United Nations resolutions which call upon it to do so. Thirty-seven per cent of the island is under military occupation by the Turkish army and the 200,000 Greek Cypriot refugees are not allowed to return to their homes in the north of Cyprus.

Consequently this book deals only with the free southern part of the island. It is the writer's and publishers' greatest wish that the unity of this beautiful country will be restored with the withdrawal of the Turkish army.

In spite of enormous trials and tribulations and centuries of foreign occupation, the people of Cyprus have not only survived for 9,000 turbulent years but have come through it all with their creativity, humanity and warmth intact.

IT IS TO THEM THAT THIS BOOK IS DEDICATED.

INTRODUCTION

The Mediterranean island of Cyprus is known internationally for two very different reasons. First and foremost it is an extremely popular holiday destination, thanks to its excellent warm climate, wonderfully hospitable people, first-rate accommodation, delicious cuisine and its safe, friendly environment. And yet many will also be aware of the fact that Cyprus is a divided island, following the 1974 Turkish Invasion, and has required the presence of a United Nations Peacekeeping Force for almost 25 years.

This curious contrast of images is repeated time and again in countless aspects of Cyprus and its people, and although many of the tourists who come here do not feel the urge to explore the innumerable fascinating facets of the island and its inhabitants, those who do make the effort to visit the various towns and villages, archaeological sites and monuments, will find that their stay is infinitely richer for it. We hope that this book will tempt you out of your hotel or apartment and into the daily lives of the Cypriot people whose long and often stormy history is certainly worth investigating through the island's museums and ancient stones.

Cyprus (population approximately 620,000) is the third largest island in the Mediterranean, located in the Eastern corner, some 60 km from Turkey to the North and 90 km from Syria to the East. Its geographical position is largely responsible for the climate which, to many visitors, seems to divide the year into nine months of Summer and three of Spring. Autumn and Winter do exist but the rainy season is short whilst snow falls only on the highest mountains in January or February. The island's location, however, also lies at the root of Cyprus' turbulent history. Standing at the crossroads, as it were, of Europe, Asia and Africa, the country has been viewed over the centuries as a strategically important stronghold by a long succession of conquerors.

The known history of Cyprus dates back over 9000 years. The foundations of small, beehive-shaped houses, evidence of a Neolithic settlement (7000-6000 B.C.), may be visited at Khirokitia, whilst finds from the site are on display at the Cyprus Museum in Nicosia. By 3000 B.C. stone tools and weapons had been replaced by implements fashioned from copper which was found in abundance. Some believe that the name "Cyprus" is derived the Latin word for cooper, "Cuprus". The island's trade in copper made it one of the busiest commercial centres in the Mediterranean.

Around 1300 B.C. Mycenean Greek traders arrived in Cyprus and founded kingdoms which grew prosperous and important. Once thriving, however, the island was to become the target of a large number of invaders and conquerors including the Assyrians, the Persians, the Ptolemies of Egypt, the Romans, the Byzantines, the self-styled Emperor Isaac Comnenos, Richard I ("The Lionheart") of England, the Knights Templar, the Lusignans and the Venetians. In 1571

Cyprus was invaded and captured by the Turks and it remained a Turkish province until 1878 when Britain took over the administration of the island. In 1923 Turkey gave up its claim to Cyprus by the Treaty of Lausanne and two years later the island became a crown colony.

Under British rule it began to prosper but the Cypriot people, of whom 80 % were Greek Cypriots, became restless under yet another foreign government and a movement for "Enosis" or Union with Greece began to gain ground. In 955, following repeated refusal by successive British governments to consider "Enosis" or independence, an armed struggle against colonial rule was begun.

In 1960 Cyprus became an independent republic, with the charismatic Archbishop Makarios III as the island's first President. Britain retained sovereign rights over an area of 150 square kilometres, with military bases at Akrotiri and Episkopi in the West and at Dhekelia in the East. Britain, Greece and Turkey became guarantors of the new state's independence.

It soon became clear that the constitution of the Republic was impractical and virtually unworkable, but when, in 1963, President Makarios proposed thirteen amendments to the constitution these were rejected by the Turkish-Cypriots, who make up approximately 18 % of the population and further than that withdrew from the government and from parliament. Between 1963 and 1974 talks between the two communities were held in an effort to find a mutually acceptable formula but the situation was dramatically altered in July 1974 when the military junta that was ruling Greece at the time staged a coup d'etat against Makarios. The President escaped with his life but the Turkish government did not fail to capitalise on this long awaited opportunity. Turkey purporting to act under the Treaty of Guarantee ordered its forces to attack. On 20th July, the first landings began and by mid August the Turkish troops had effectively sealed off the northern sector of the island, some 37 % of its territory. The Turkish invasion caused heavy loss of life both in the course of military occupations and in attacks on civilians by the Turkish troops. Not long after the bloody invasion illegal immigrants from Turkey have been brought into the northern occupied part of the island. Cyprus, still remains illegaly divided by the military forces of Turkey to date.

The tourist who visits the government-held part of Cyprus is unlikely to be aware of the situation unless he or she approached to so-called "Green Line" in Nicosia or talks with the many Cypriots who lost relatives and friends during the 1974 invasion. The South of the island is thriving economically and tourism figures improve from one year to another. This book refers only to those areas which are accessible to everyone. There is much to see and enjoy on "Aphrodite's Island" as Euripides described it almost two and a half thousand years ago, and although many things have changed since then, the magic is still there.

Nicosia

NICOSIA is the capital city of Cyprus and the largest on the island with a population in the Southern sector of some 120,000. It is the only sizeable inland town and it houses the main government offices as well as the headquarters of many major local and international companies. The Presidential Palace is in Nicosia which is a busy commercial centre today.

The capital, (in Greek called "Lefkosia", most probably after its founder, Lefkon, son of Ptolemy I) lies close to the ancient site of Ledra. It grew in size in the 7th Century when people from the coastal areas moved inland to escape attacks by neighbouring countries and quickly became the most important city in Cyprus.

The walls which enclose the old part of the city were constructed by the Venetians to withstand an expected invasion by the Turks in 1570. They were strengthened by eleven bastions and a birds-eye view of the circular wall today features in the city's official emblem. Entry was by three gates, one of which is still used today, though no longer as a crossing point.

The FAMAGUSTA GATE, once the main entrance to Nicosia, is now a cultural centre and the venue for exhibitions, lectures, plays and concerts. The beautifully restored vaults of the original gate are worth seeing for themselves.

Nicosia's main attraction for visitors is the CYPRUS MUSEUM, built as a memorial to Queen Victoria, contains a rich collection of finds from all over the island. Although Cyprus is full of relics from as far back as the Neolithic era, interest in archaeology did not really begin until the 19th Century. It was then that a number of foreign diplomats engaged in "treasure hunts" in order to enrich their own private collections, the most famous of all being General Louis Palma di Cesnola, American Consul in Cyprus, who excavated extensively between 1865 and 1878. He collected thousands of antiquities from all over the island and sold most of them to the Metropolitan Museum in New York. The so-called "Curium Treasure" is part of this collection.

Prior to the building of the present Cyprus Museum, which began in 1908, an earlier museum had been set up in a house in Nicosia. In the 1930s the newly-established museum was enriched with finds from several important excavations, in particular from the Swedish-Cyprus Expedition (1927-31). Swedish professor Einar Gjerstad is usually honoured as the founder of the scientific approach to archaeology in Cyprus.

Since 1960 a new awareness has developed in Cyprus regarding the island's archaeological heritage. Foreign missions and excavations by the Department of Antiquities, under the enlightened guidance of its Director, Dr Vasos Karageorghis, have continued to unearth significant artefacts and reveal more secrets of the island's fascinating past.

Across the road from the museum stands the MUNICIPAL THEATRE, a modern building constructed on classical lines. It is used throughout the year for concerts and other cultural events and is the permanent home of the Cyprus National Theatre.

The ARCHBISHOP'S PALACE is an impressive three storey building, a modern

The 1974 Cyprus Tragedy monument at Akaki (near Nicosia).

construction in Venetian style, liked by some visitors though others find it vulgar. Apart from being the official residence of the Archbishop of Cyprus, it also houses the Makarios III Cultural Foundation. This contains three art galleries, including the superb BYZANTINE MUSEUM, a unique collection of Byzantine icons, representing the full range of Byzantine painting.

Next to the Archbishop's Palace is ST. JOHN'S CATHEDRAL, built in 1665 on the site of a former Benedictine Abbey. Its interior is covered with wall paintings of the 18th Century.

On the other side of the church stand the old monastery buildings. These used to be known as the old Archbishopric and are now the home of the FOLK ART MUSEUM. It contains traditional costumes, domestic utensils, lace, woodcarvings, pottery, paintings and so on.

The NATIONAL STRUGGLE MUSEUM gathers together a collection of photographs, documents and weapons used during the struggle against British colonial rule in 1955 by the E.O.K.A. organisation. It is of considerable interest to those who wish to learn more about the modern history of Cyprus.

ELEFTHERIA SQUARE is the city's chief venue for large, outdoor gatherings. It lies at the entrance to Ledra Street which was once the main shopping street of Nicosia and remains a busy, though narrow thoroughfare today. Although noisy and often congested traffic passes constantly through Eleftheria Square, peace and tranquility reign only a few steps away in the LAIKI YITONIA or "Popular Neighbourhood". The streets and houses in this area were restored and renovated a few years ago to give the impression of Nicosia in the 1920s and thereby recreate the atmosphere of a bygone era. There are small boutiques, workshops, tavernas and cafes here and the quarter is both picturesque and relaxing.

The craftsmen are happy to let you watch them at work, but for a large collection of local handicrafts, the CYPRUS HANDICRAFTS CENTRE is the place to go. Built in 1980 at the entrance to Nicosia as a place for refugee craftsmen and women to work, it contains a number of workshops which may be visited and has an excellent range of pottery, carved wood, woven materials, lace and copper objects on sale. The government-run Centre also has branches in the other towns of the island.

Laiki Yitonia

Top left *The Old Archbishopric-Folk Art Museum.* **Top right** *The National Struggle Museum.* **Bottom** *Interior of the Folk Art Museum.*
Opposite *Statue of an E.O.K.A. fighter outside the National Struggle Museum.*

Top left *Eleftheria Square.* **Top right** *"Severios" Library.* **Bottom/Opposite** *The Famagusta Gate.*

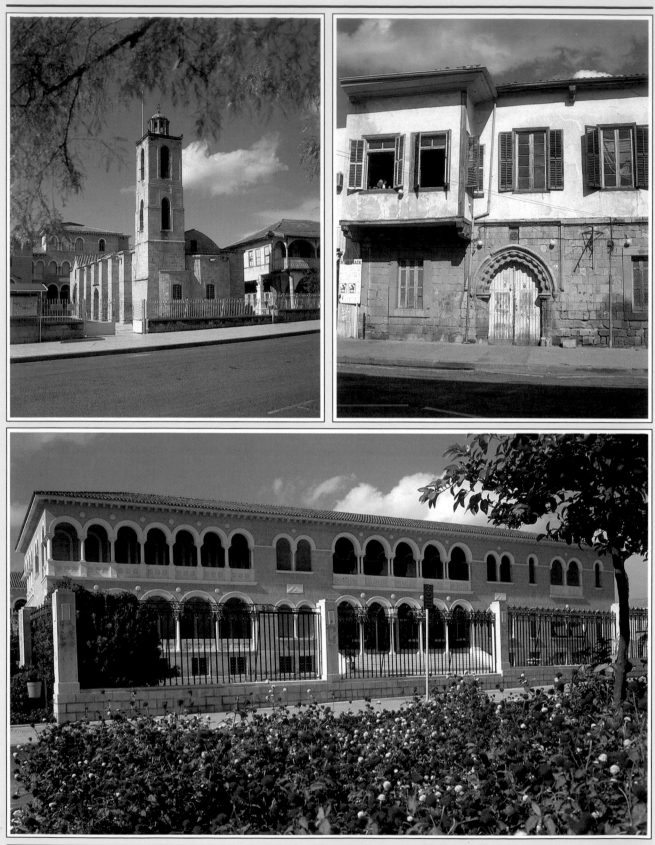

Top left *St. John's Cathedral.* **Top right** *A restored house of the late 19th century.* **Bottom** *The Archbishop's Palace.*
Opposite *The monument to Archbishop Kyprianos.*

Top *The 16th century Venetian Walls.* **Bottom** *The Municipal Theatre.* **Opposite** *A typical restored house in the Laiki Yitonia.*

Top left *Marble head of statue of Artemis (2nd century A.D.).* **Top right** *Openwork ivory plaque, depicting a winged Sphinx found in Salamis* (750-600 B.C.).* **Bottom** *Marble statue of sleeping Eros (1st century A.D.).* **Opposite** *The entrance to the Cyprus Museum in Nicosia.*
All ancient finds shown in this book are exhibited at the Cyprus Museum.

Top left *Cult vessel decorated with animal protomes (2075-2000 B.C.).* **Bottom left** *Reconstruction of an ancient tomb.* **Right** *Bronze statuette of the Horned God from Engomi* (12th century B.C.).* **Opposite** *Marble statue of Aphrodite (1st century B.C.).*
*Locations marked with an asterisk are presently under Turkish military occupation.

Top left *Stirrup jar of Proto Bichrome ware (11th century B.C.).* **Top right** *Anthropomorphic stone idol from Khirokitia (7000-6000 B.C.). This is one of the most ancient finds in Cyprus.* **Bottom left** *Composite vase with a female figurine attached to the neck (17th century B.C.).* **Bottom right** *Mycenaean crater with bull representations (13th century B.C.).* **Opposite** *Terracota figurine of a horseman (750-600 B.C.).*

Top left *Limestone head of a female statue (600-475 B.C.).* **Bottom left** *Limestone statuette of Zeus Keraunios, The Thunderer (5th century B.C.).* **Right** *Cruciform steatite idol (3500-2300 B.C.).* **Opposite** *Mosaic "emblem" depicting "Leda and the Swan" (3rd century A.D.).*

Top/Bottom left *Limassol Carnival.* **Right** *Wine Festival.* **Opposite** *Aerial view of Limassol.*

Top left *Boat cruise off the Limassol coastline.* **Bottom left** *Sunset at ancient Amathus.* **Right** *A restored Inn north of Limassol.* **Opposite** *An old boat at Dasoudhi beach.*

Top left *Dasoudhi beach*. **Top right** *Old port quay*. **Bottom** *Aerial view of Limassol and the Old Port*. **Opposite** *Aerial view of Dasoudhi beach*.

Top left *Interior of Limassol Castle.* **Top right** *The cemetery Chapel at Ayios Yeoryios Alamanos.* **Bottom** *Yermasoyia dam in spring (near Limassol).* **Opposite** *Flocks grazing at Yermasoyia dam.*

The Sanctuary of Apollo Hylates. **Opposite** *The Curium Amphitheatre.*

The Sanctuary of Apollo Hylates.

Impressive mosaic details in the Villa of Eustolios at Ancient Curium. **Opposite** *The magnificent floor mosaic in the villa of Eustolios depicting Ktisis (Creation).*

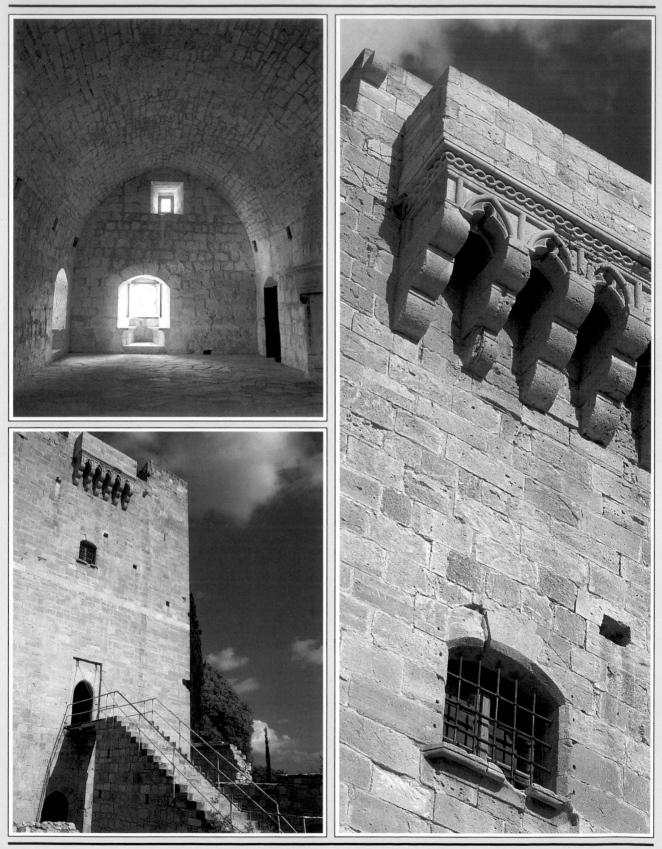

Kolossi Castle. **Opposite** *Spectacular view of the Mediterranean sea from the Kourion Cliffs.*

Kolossi Castle. **Opposite** *Interior of the Old Sugar Refinery at Kolossi.*

Petra Tou Romiou or Rock of Aphrodite: The legendary Birthplace of the ancient Greek Goddess of Love who rose from the waves.

Top *Pissouri Bay.* **Bottom** *The picturesque harbour at Kato Paphos.* **Opposite** *The Pelican at Kato Paphos harbour.*

Top left *The mediaeval church at Polis.* **Top right** *The rocky side of Coral Bay.* **Bottom left** *The crystal clear waters near the Baths of Aphrodite.* **Bottom right** *The sandy side of Coral Bay.* **Opposite** *The church of Ayios Yeoryios (Khlorakas).*

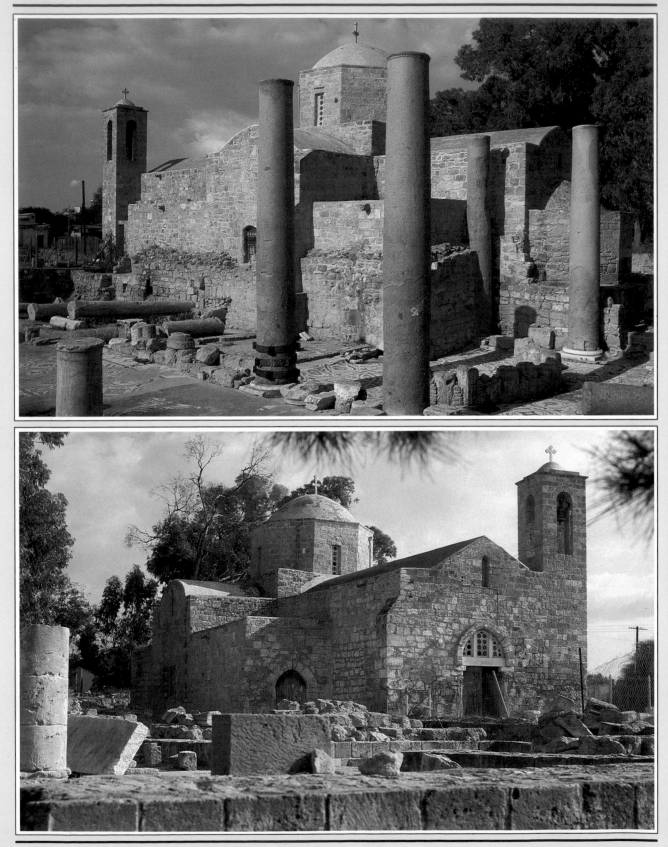

Top *St. Paul's Pillars.* **Bottom** *The Basilica of Ayia Kyriaki (Chrysopolitissa).* **Opposite** *The ancient ruins at Kato Paphos.*

The ancient site around the Basilica of Ayia Kyriaki. **Opposite** *Tombs of the Kings.*

Top *The 13th century Chateau De Covocle (Kouklia).* **Bottom** *The Odeon (Kato Paphos).* **Opposite** *The Ancient ruins of Aphrodite's Temple (Kouklia).*

Larnaca

*LARNACA is likely to give visitors their first impressions of Cyprus
since the island's largest International Airport is here.
It has flourished as a tourist resort over the past ten years
and is the third largest town in Cyprus,
though with some 30,000 inhabitants it is much smaller than Nicosia and Limassol.
Most of the Northern part of the town stands on the site of ancient Kition,
one of whose illustrious sons was the Philosopher Zeno (335-263 B.C.)*

The CHURCH OF ST. LAZARUS is Larnaca's most impressive old building. It stands on the site of the original 9th Century church, which itself was built over the tomb of Lazarus whom Christ resurrected. Lazarus is said to have sailed to Kition where he eventually died. The building which stands today was erected in the 17th Century. Inside the church, which has three aisles and three domes, you will see icons, silver furnishings and carved woodwork. St. Lazarus' tomb is in the crypt under the church.

The PIERIDES MUSEUM is another place of interest, especially to amateur archaeologists and historians. It contains a large collection of archaeological finds amassed by the family of Demetrios Pierides (1811-1895), and the thousands of objects on show span Cypriot history from Neolithic to Byzantine times.

LARNACA PROMENADE, known locally as "Phinikoudhes" ("Palms") after the trees that line the sea front, is a popular meeting and walking place with the local people. Beyond it stands the Turkish fort built in 1625 and now used as a museum for finds from Kition and other sites. One can walk along the walls which afford good views of the sea.

Some 4 Km from Larnaca in the direction of the airport is the HALA SULTAN TEKKE, an important Muslim shrine which is said to contain the remains of Hala Sultan, the maternal aunt of the Prophet Mohammed. The mosque was built in her honour by the Turks in 1816. Located amid rich greenery it is an impressive sight, especially when viewed across the Salt Lake.

At Kiti, to the West of Larnaca town, is the famous church of PANAYIA ANGELOKTISTOS ("built by Angels"). This 11th Century building replaced an earlier one, whilst the chapel at the entrance is of the 14th Century. The outstanding feature of the church is its splendid early Byzantine mosaic, considered to be the finest on the island. The only similar one is in the church of Kanakaria in the occupied Karpass district. The church is certainly worth visiting for the mosaic alone.

The OLD AQUEDUCT was built in 1745 to provide Larnaca with water. It was the largest of three and is known in Greek as "Kamares" which means "Arches". It dominates the landscape on the Larnaca-Limassol road 3 Km from the town.

KHIROKITIA is the oldest site that one may visit in Cyprus today (an older one lies in the occupied Karpass Peninsula), and it dates back to Neolithic times (7000-6000 B.C). Discovered in 1934 this significant site revealed numerous stone foundations of bee-hive shaped houses, usually circular. The houses themselves would have been of

"Kamares" - The old Aqueduct.

mud brick and the ancient inhabitants of Khirokitia buried their dead under the floors of their dwellings. As many as 26 adult and infant skeletons have been discovered beneath 8 superimposed floors in one of the houses. The site lies off the main Nicosia-Limassol road, whilst many of the finds are in the Cyprus Museum in Nicosia.

Left *Larnaca Marina.* **Top right** *General view of Larnaca.* **Bottom right** *The Neolithic settlement of Khirokitia.* **Opposite** *The Larnaca Promenade, known locally as "Phinikoudes" - ("Palms").*

Top left/right *Larnaca Castle/Museum.* **Bottom left** *The impressive interior of St. Lazarus church.* **Bottom right** *Larnaca castle.* **Opposite** *The church of St. Lazarus.*

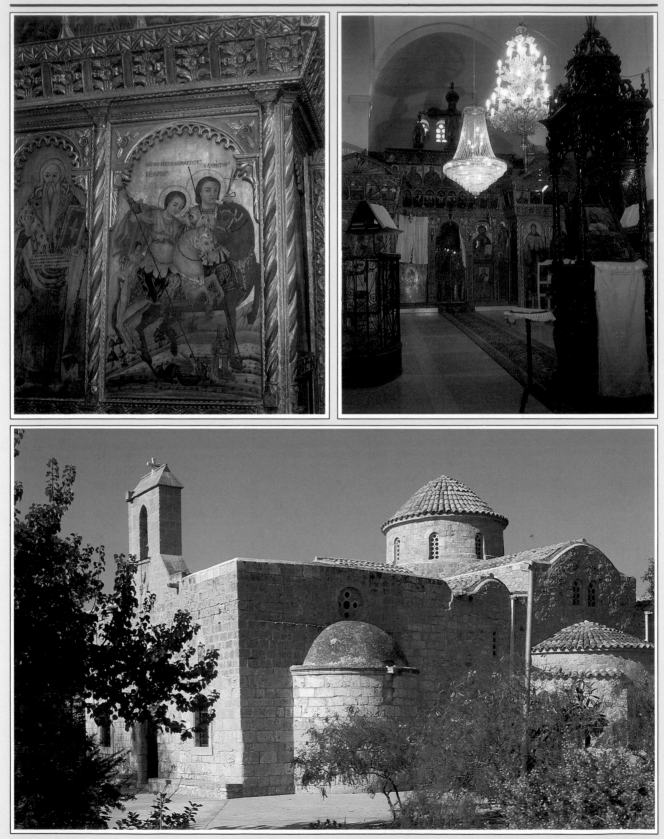

The church and interior of Panayia Angeloktistos. **Opposite** *The outstanding Byzantine mosaic that depicts The Virgin and the Child, flanked by Archangels Gabriel and Michael; it dates from between 5th and 9th centuries (Angeloktistos-Kiti).*

Ayia Napa

*Ten years ago AYIA NAPA was a sleepy fishing village,
noted for its 16th Century monastery.
Today it is arguably the busiest of all the island's seaside resorts
and much development has taken place to provide accommodation and services
for the thousands of visitors that throng the area in Summer.*

In the centre of the village lies the MONASTERY OF AYIA NAPA, built by the Venetians behind strong stone walls. There is an attractive marble fountain covered by a dome resting on four pillars in the courtyard. The church of the monastery is partly underground and is entered by descending a flight of steps. From the small Latin chapel one can go down to the 600 year old Sycamore tree which stands next to a large cistern.

The sandy beaches of Ayia Napa resemble those of the now-inaccessible Famagusta and are a major attraction, those of Nissi Beach, Makronisos Beach, Sandy Beach and Ayia Napa Main Beach being the most popular. Eight kilometres to the East in the area known as Protaras lies another well-known beauty spot, that of Fig Tree Bay, famous for its wonderfully clear water and golden sands.

The Protaras area is dotted with windmills and visitors tend to cycle rather than walk or drive along the narrow roads. Not far from' Cape Greco the CHURCH OF PROPHITIS ELIAS perched high on an outcrop of rock, close to which a very attractive "holiday village" has been built.

Close to the village of Xylophagou, three kilometres west of Ayia Napa, is the picturesque fishing shelter of Potamos which is certainly worth a visit.

Ayia Napa is rapidly becoming as popular with the Cypriots as it is with foreign tourists as a holiday resort and the scenery of the district is changing all the time as new hotels and apartment blocks go up. The danger of over-development is not far away but it is hoped that the area's traditional character will not be sacrificed for commercial ends.

Ayia Napa Main beach.

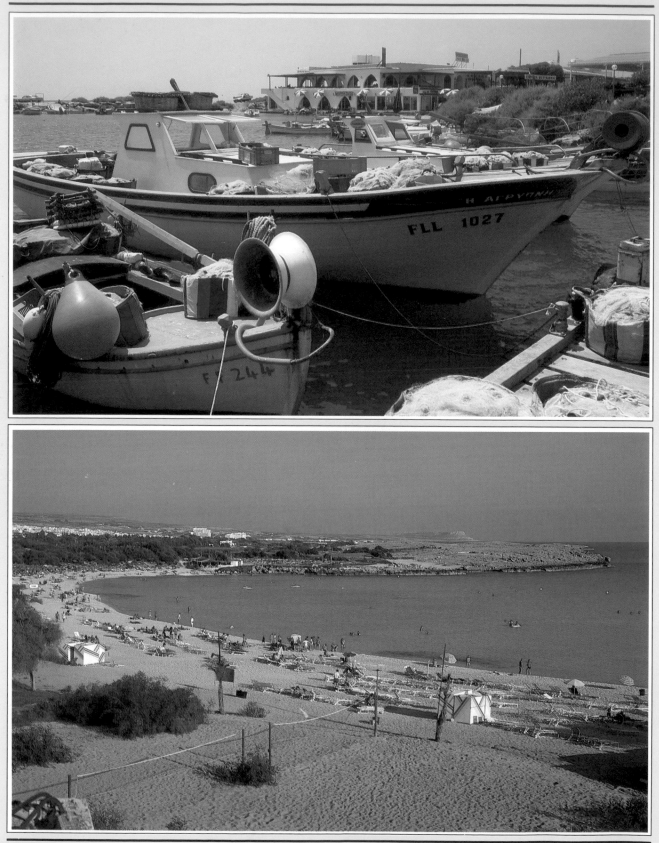

Top *Ayia Napa fishing harbour.* **Bottom** *Nissi beach.* **Opposite** *Fishing boats at the harbour.*

The Monastery of Ayia Napa with its famous domed fountain.

Top *The fishing shelter at Potamos (Xylophagou).* **Bottom** *The ruined domed church of Ayios Theodhoros.* **Opposite** *The 12th century church of Ayios Yeoryios.*

Top left/right *Fig Tree bay.* **Bottom left** *The church of Prophitis Elias (Protaras).* **Bottom right** *Protaras beach.* **Opposite** *The famous windmills of Protaras.*

Mountain Villages

Although the mountain villages of Cyprus are sparsely populated nowadays, many of them are transformed into bustling holiday resorts in the Summer when the inhabitants of Nicosia and Limassol in particular take to the hills to escape the heat of July and August.

PLATRES, a favourite with Limassolians, is active almost all the year round and contains a number of hotels, shops and restaurants. Partially hidden on a wooded hillside it is about 45 minutes by car from Limassol. Platres is at its busiest in the Summer when an annual Festival is held there.

When travelling from Limassol to Platres it is worth leaving the main road to visit the pretty village of LANIA. On the road itself stands the ROYAL OAK, a tree which is reputed to be over 1,000 years old. Turning left off the Limassol-Platres road immediately before the Lania turnoff one comes to the village of MONAGRI. It was once celebrated for the now deserted monastery of ARCHANGELOS MICHAEL.

TROODOS is not a village, but a collection of cafes, shops and one or two hotels which are used in Winter when skiers flock to the mountains to enjoy the snow. It lies just below the island's highest peak, Mount Olympus (1,950 m above sea level) and an annual tennis tournament attracts visitors in Summer. All the year round Troodos is a pleasant spot for walks. Five miles to the South, on the way to Platres, is Government Lodge, the President's Summer home. It is notable for the fact that the celebrated French poet Arthur Rimbaud worked on its construction and there is a plaque to commemorate this.

KAKOPETRIA, like Platres, is a favourite resort. Usually it is populated in the Summer by visitors from Nicosia who appreciate its shady corners. There are plenty of picturesque old houses, an ancient flour mill and some excellent restaurants.

Some 5 km from Platres is PHINI, a charming little village famous for its red clay pottery. It is also the location of a privately-run Folk Art Museum. The owner, Mr. Pilavakis, and his wife are always delighted to show visitors around.

A mile from Phini stands the MONASTERY OF AYII ANARGYRI. The church, which is probably of the 15th Century, is said to be haunted.

The village of OMODHOS lies 6 km from Platres and is famous for its vineyards, its lace and an annual Wine Festival. The Byzantine church of the MONASTERY OF STAVROS which used to stand in the middle of the village was replaced and then rebuilt in the 1930s. The key to the monastery door is reputed to be the largest in Cyprus.

PANAYIA in the Paphos district is famous as the birthplace of Archbishop Makarios III, the first President of Cyprus. The house where he lived as a boy is now a small museum.

STAVROS TIS PSOKAS is a forest station which was established in 1884. It has a resthouse and a restaurant, and several mouflon, the wild sheep of Cyprus, may be seen here in protected confinement.

LEFKARA, nestling in the foothills of the Troodos Mountains, is renowned for its "Lefkaritika" or Lefkara Lace. The name is,

Mountain village scene.

in fact, incorrect since this "lace" is actually linen with drawn embroidery inserts. It has been well-known for centuries and it is said that Leonardo da Vinci visited Lefkara in 1481 and bought "Lefkaritika" for the altar of Milan Cathedral. Lefkara today is a pretty village where one still sees the women sewing in the courtyards of their homes as their mothers and grandmothers did before them.

Top *Old Kakopetria.* **Bottom left** *The deserted monastery of Archangelos Michael (Monagri).* **Bottom right** *Lania village.*
Opposite *The remains of an old bridge near Monagri village.*

Top *Phini village.* **Bottom** *The 15th century monastery of Ayii Anargyri (Phini).* **Opposite** *An example of the famous Phini redclay pottery.*

Top/Bottom left *The Phini Folk Art Museum.* **Bottom right** *Grandmother remembers.* **Opposite** *A ninety year old villager wearing the traditional "vraka"*

Top *The door to the Monastery of Stavros (Omodhos).* **Bottom** *The key to the Stavros Monastery door, reputed to be the largest in Cyprus.*
Opposite *Omodhos village.*

Interior of the house at Panayia where Archbishop Makarios III was born and lived as a boy. **Opposite** *The statue of Archbishop Makarios III.*

The birthplace of Archbishop Makarios III (Panayia). **Opposite** *Cyprus Pine: The predominant tree on the Troodos mountains.*

Top left/Opposite *"Lefkaritika" or Lefkara Lace: The art of making the world famous embroidery has been passed on from one generation to another for centuries.* **Top right** *Lefkara High School.* **Bottom** *Lefkara village.*

Churches

*Many of the old churches of Cyprus are famous for their exquisite frescoes,
a great number of which are extremely well-preserved or have been restored.
Some of the most interesting are the following:*

CHURCH OF AYIOS NICHOLAS TIS STEYIS

This is one of the best-known Byzantine churches on the island. It was built in the 11th Century though alterations over the centuries have changed its appearance considerably. At the end of the 1300s a second roof was added to the church, concealing the dome and vaults. This roof gave it its present name ("Steyis" means "roof"). It contains wall paintings from the 11th to the 15th centuries and a 17th century iconostasis.

CHURCH OF PANAYIA TIS PODITHOU

This church, which stands just outside the village of Galata, is one of the most important wooden roofed churches in the Troodos area. The roof reaches almost to the ground whilst the four windows which were opened 30 years ago in order to provide more light inside have given the church a slightly different appearance from the original. An inscription beneath one of the paintings tells us that the church was founded in 1502. It was never completely decorated but the frescoes which were painted were highly influenced by the Italian art of the time. The iconostasis was made in the 16th century and repaired in the 18th.

CHURCH OF PANAYIA TOU ARAKA

This is one of the most important churches in Cyprus. Situated near the village of La-

goudhera, it was built in the last year of the 12th century and is covered by a large dome with twelve narrow windows. Frescoes were painted on the walls in 1192 but these were damaged by damp. To prevent further damage a second steep-pitched wooden roof was added to the dome and vaults of the church. During the 18th century the West wall was demolished and the church extended. It takes its present appearance from this time. The dome, the vaults and walls of the church, apart from the later extension, are covered with 12th century frescoes.

CHURCH OF SAINTS BARNABAS AND HILARION at Peristerona

This five domed church in the Nicosia district is similar in many ways to that of Ayia Paraskevi at Yeroskipou. It is built of roughly squared sandstone and is high, despite the heavy domes.

It was constructed at the beginning of the 12th century, and although only remnants of the frescoes with which it was decorated remain, some beautiful icons and carved 16th century doors are preserved in the church. Also exhibited inside are mediaeval tombstones and bronze plates as well as a very old carved chest depicting a town under siege.

CHURCH OF PANAYIA TIS ASINOU

The best-known of all the old painted

The church of Archangelos Michael (Galata).

churches of Cyprus, it was built at the beginning of the 12th Century as the church of the Monastery of Phorbia, and was originally known as Phorbiotissa. Its present name came from the nearby township of Asine. It was decorated with frescoes in 1105 and new ones were painted in 1333. They have been cleaned and preserved and are considered by many to be the finest collection of wall paintings in Cyprus.

Top/bottom left *The church of Panayia Tis Asinou.* **Right** *The church of Saints Barnabas and Hilarion (Peristerona).* **Opposite** *The church of Ayios Nicholas Tis Steyis (Kakopetria).*

Top left/right *The church of Panayia Tis Podithou (Galata).* **Bottom left** *The domed church of Panayia Tou Araka (Lagoudhera).* **Bottom right** *The church of Ayia Paraskevi (Galata).* **Opposite** *Old wall paintings from the church of Ayia Paraskevi (Galata).*

ΑΘΑΝΆΣΙΟΣ ΠΑΘ ΙΩ

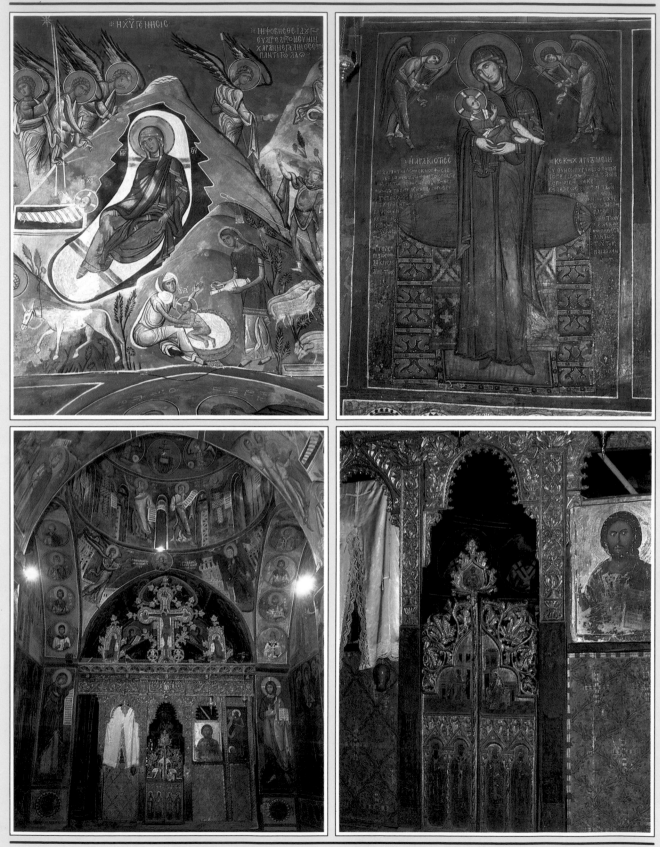

The superb 12th century frescoes from the church of Panayia Tou Araka (Lagoudhera). **Bottom right** *The iconostasis of Panayia Tou Araka (Lagoudhera).*

The superb 12th century frescoes from the church of Panayia Tou Araka (Lagoudhera).

Monasteries

*Cyprus has a large number of monasteries,
many of which are situated in superb mountain areas
with breathtaking views.*

The Royal KYKKOS MONASTERY, founded in 1080 by Byzantine Emperor Alexios Komnenos, is certainly the most famous of all the monasteries of the island and is known throughout the Orthodox world. Located some 1,200 metres above sea level, Kykkos took its name from the hillside on which it was built. It was granted autonomy by its founder who also donated one of the three surviving icons of the Virgin Mary reputed to have been painted by St. Luke himself. The Emperor Komnenos also handed over estates and property to assist in the financial upkeep of the monastery.

It is recorded in manuscripts that in the 14th Century four hundred monks lived within the monastery. In its nine hundred years of existence it has burnt down four times, the last time in 1813. The icon of the Virgin Mary has survived to this day and is now completely covered with silver gilt plate. It is believed to have miraculous rainmaking powers.

A small but interesting museum may be visited at the monastery. It contains all the precious items and treasures that have survived the fires and which escaped the looting by the Turks in 1821. Today the Monastery of Kykkos is a popular place of pilgrimage for Cypriots and tourists alike.

Two kilometres uphill is THRONI (the Seat of the Virgin Mary). Close to this holy monument is the site of the tomb Archbishop Makarios III. Makarios was not only the first President of Cyprus but a leading member of the Kykkos brotherhood, and he personally chose the location of his tomb. It has a spectacular view across Cyprus and faces his birthplace, the village of Panayia. Since Makarios' death in 1977, Throni has become an additional place of pilgrimage for all visitors to Kykkos Monastery.

MACHERAS MONASTERY is located 30 miles from Nicosia and stands 900 meters above sea level on an impressive site with excellent views. It was founded in the 12th Century by two monks who are said to have discovered an icon of the Virgin Mary in a nearby cave. The monastery burned down twice, the second time in 1892, and little of the original building remains. The hideout in which E.O.K.A. here Grigoris Afxentiou died in 1957 is preserved nearby.

Perched 700 meters above sea level on top of a rocky peak, STAVROVOUNI MONASTERY ("The Mountain on the Cross") affords wonderful views of the Troodos hills and the South coast. Founded in 327 A.D., reputedly by St. Helena who is said to have brought a piece of the True Cross with her, the monastery was destroyed several times. The present building dates from the 17th Century. Note that women are not allowed to enter the church of the monastery.

Seven miles from Paphos is the MONASTERY OF ST. NEOPHYTOS, founded by the Saint around the year 1200. Neophytos was born in the village of Lefkara and was a scholar and author. He carved out his hermitage ("Engleistra") in the rock and later personally oversaw the walll painting. The monastery grew up next to the caves where

The Royal Kykkos Monastery.

he lived for 40 years. These lie just West of the 15th Century domed church and monastery buildings. The Saint's bones were removed from his tomb in 1750 and are kept in a wooden sarcophagus in the church.

Situated near the village of Panayia, birthplace of Archibishop Makarios III, the MONASTERY OF PANAYIA CHRYSOROYIATISSA ("Our Lady of the Golden Pomegranite") was founded in 1152 by a monk named Ignatius. The present church dates from the 18th Century, though some repairs were carried out in 1955. Ignatius is said to have found an icon of the Virgin Mary in the sea and carried it to the mountains. In a dream the Virgin told him to set the icon down and build a monastery there. The icon is kept in the monastery.

The MONASTERY OF TROODITISSA, set high in the Troodos mountains between Platres and Prodhrómos, was founded in 1250. This is the third church to be built on the site and dates from 1731, although some restoration was carried out in the 1960s. The holy icon of the Virgin Mary, for which the monastery is said to have been built, was covered in silver plate in 1799.

The most famous relic in the monastery is the Holy Belt, said to make childress women fertile.

Top left *A modern mosaic at Kykkos Monastery.* **Top right** *Monks' Chambers at Kykkos.* **Bottom** *The inner courtyard of Kykkos Monastery.* **Opposite** *Byzantine style contemporary frescoes in the Kykkos Monastery.*

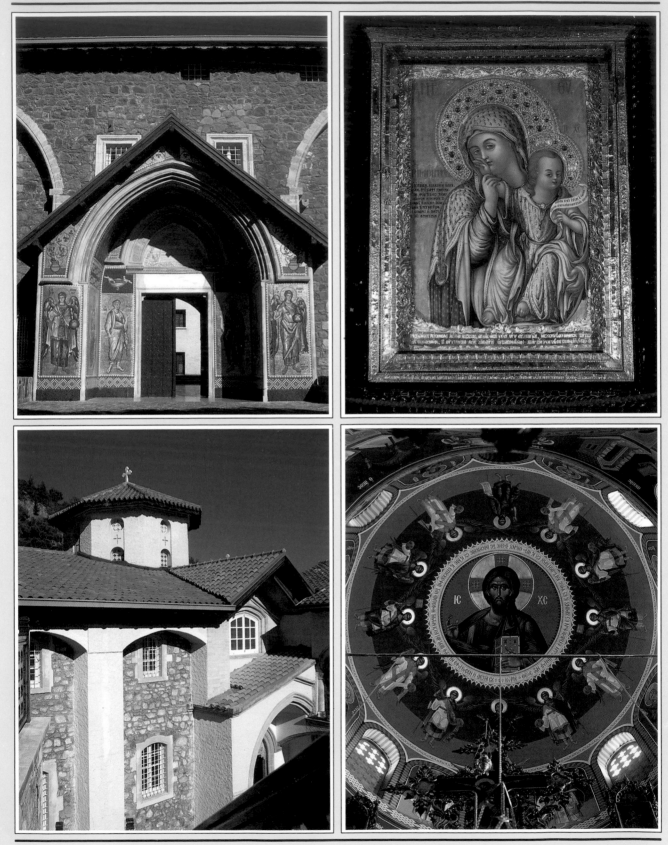

Top left *Entrance to Kykkos Monastery.* **Top right** *An old icon, painted in 1801 by the Cretan artist Ioannis Cornaros.*
Bottom left/right *The dome and its painted interior.* **Opposite** *Interior of the Royal Kykkos Monastery showing the magnificent frescoes in the Byzantine style, painted by the contemporary Cypriot artist Georgios Georgiou.*

Top left/right *Old Wooden Press and Millstone outside the Kykkos Monastery.* **Bottom** *The Tomb of Archbishop Makarios (Throni).*
Opposite *Contemporary frescoes in the Byzantine style of Kykkos Monastery.*

Top left/opposite *The Monastery of St. Neophytos.* **Top right** *The "Engleistra": St. Neophytos, Hermitage.* **Bottom left/right** *"Engleistra" old frescoes.*

Macheras Monastery.

Monastery of Trooditissa. **Opposite** *Stavrovouni Monastery.*

Top *Detail of the Monastery of Panayia Chrysoroyiatissa.* **Bottom** *A young monk resting with his donkey after a hard day's work.*
Opposite *The Monastery of Panayia Chrysoroyiatissa.* **Last page** *A lifetime devoted to God.*